How To Use This Study Guide

This five-lesson study guide corresponds to *"Earnestly Contending for the Faith" With Rick Renner* (Renner TV). Each lesson in this study guide covers a topic that is addressed during the program series, with questions and references supplied to draw you deeper into your own private study of the Scriptures on this subject.

To derive the most benefit from this study guide, consider the following:

First, watch or listen to the program prior to working through the corresponding lesson in this guide. (Programs can also be viewed at **renner.org** by clicking on the Media/Archives links or on our Renner Ministries YouTube channel.)

Second, take the time to look up the scriptures included in each lesson. Prayerfully consider their application to your own life.

Third, use a journal or notebook to make note of your answers to each lesson's Study Questions and Practical Application challenges.

Fourth, invest specific time in prayer and in the Word of God to consult with the Holy Spirit. Write down the scriptures or insights He reveals to you.

Finally, take action! Whatever the Lord tells you to do according to His Word, do it.

For added insights on this subject, it is recommended that you obtain Rick Renner's book *How To Keep Your Head on Straight in a World Gone Crazy: Developing Discernment for These Last Days*. You may also select from Rick's other available resources by placing your order at **renner.org** or by calling 1-800-742-5593.

LESSON 1

TOPIC
What It Means To Be a Servant of God

SCRIPTURES
1. **Jude 1** — Jude, the servant of Jesus Christ, and brother of James, to them that are sanctified [loved] by God the Father, and preserved [kept] in Jesus Christ, and called.

GREEK WORDS
1. "servant" — δοῦλος (*doulos*): the most abject term for a slave; depicts one who is totally sold into slavery and who is a slave for life; one bound to do the bidding of his owner and whose reason for existence is to help, assist, and fulfill his master's wants and dreams to the exclusion of all else; a servant who lives to serve in whatever way the master asks or demands, hence, one whose will is completely swallowed up in the will of his master
2. "brother" — ἀδελφός (*adelphos*): two or more who were born from the same womb; popularized at the time of Alexander the Great in a military sense to depict comrades in battle; used here to describe Jude's natural-born relationship to James, who was the author of the epistle of James and was the leader of the church in Jerusalem; James and Jude were also the half-brothers of Jesus
3. "sanctified"/"loved" — ἀγάπη (*agape*): a divine love that gives, even if it's never responded to, thanked, or acknowledged; a love that causes a viewer to behold an object or person in esteem, awe, admiration, wonder, and appreciation and awakens such great respect in the heart of the observer for the object or person being beheld that he is compelled to love it; a love for a person or object that is irresistible and so profound that it knows no limits or boundaries in how far, wide, high, and deep it will go to show that love to its recipient; a self-sacrificial love that moves the lover to action

A Note From Rick Renner

I am on a personal quest to see a "revival of the Bible" so people can establish their lives on a firm foundation that will stand strong and endure the test as end-time storm winds begin to intensify.

In order to experience a revival of the Bible in your personal life, it is important to take time each day to read, receive, and apply its truths to your life. James tells us that if we will continue in the perfect law of liberty — refusing to be forgetful hearers, but determined to be doers — we will be blessed in our ways. As you watch or listen to the programs in this series and work through this corresponding study guide, I trust you will search the Scriptures and allow the Holy Spirit to help you hear something new from God's Word that applies specifically to your life. I encourage you to be a doer of the Word He reveals to you. Whatever the cost, I assure you — it will be worth it.

> Thy words were found, and I did eat them;
> and thy word was unto me the joy and rejoicing of mine heart:
> for I am called by thy name, O Lord God of hosts.
> — Jeremiah 15:16

Your brother and friend in Jesus Christ,

Rick Renner

Rick Renner

Unless otherwise indicated, all scripture quotations are taken from the *King James Version* of the Bible.

Scripture quotations marked (*TLB*) are taken from *The Living Bible* copyright © 1971. Used by permission of Tyndale House Publishers, Inc., Carol Stream, Illinois 60188. All rights reserved.

Earnestly Contending for the Faith —
Making the Choice To Maintain Your Faith Regardless of Pressures To Modify It in These Last Days

Copyright © 2022 by Rick Renner
P.O. Box 702040
Tulsa, OK 74170

Published by Rick Renner Ministries
www.renner.org

ISBN 13: 978-1-6675-0029-4

eBook ISBN 13: 978-1-6675-0030-0

All rights reserved. No portion of this book may be reproduced or transmitted in any form or by any means — electronic, mechanical, photocopy, recording, scanning, or other — except for brief quotations in critical reviews or articles, without the prior written permission of the Publisher.

SYNOPSIS

The five lessons in this study on ***Earnestly Contending for the Faith*** will focus on the following topics:

- What It Means To Be a Servant of God
- Experiencing the Mercy, Peace, and Love of God
- What It Means To Earnestly Contend for the Faith
- God's Expectation for Us To Maintain the Purity of the Faith
- Divine Warnings

The emphasis of this lesson:

Jude was the half-brother of Jesus, the brother of James, and the son of Mary and Joseph. God called this entire family into relationship with Him and into His ministry. Rather than boast of his illustrious position as Jesus' half-brother, Jude identified himself as Jesus' servant. As believers, we are deeply embedded in Christ and greatly loved by God.

Though it is small in size, the book of Jude is packed with important truth for all believers — especially those living in these last of the last days. Acting as a First Century reporter, Jude shines a spotlight on false teachers who have snuck into the Church and have turned the grace of God into a license to sin. Who was this obscure man named Jude, and why are his words just as vital for our generation as they were for those living in the First Century? That is the focus of this first lesson.

Who Was Jude? And Who Were His Family Members?

Now you may be thinking, *Just who is this Jude fellow?* The answer is he is the half-brother of Jesus. He and Jesus had the same mother — Mary — but they had different fathers. Jude's father was Joseph, and Jesus was the Son of God the Father. Matthew 1:18 (*TLB*) says, "These are the facts concerning the birth of Jesus Christ: His mother, Mary, was engaged to be married to Joseph. But while she was still a virgin she became pregnant by the Holy Spirit." In other words, Mary was not impregnated with Jesus by Joseph; she became pregnant when the Holy Spirit came upon her and supernaturally conceived Jesus (*see* Luke 1:35).

History documents that after Jesus was born, Mary and Joseph came together as any healthy, married couple would and produced several children. In fact, Matthew 13:55 reveals that Joseph — the carpenter — and Mary were the parents of James, Joses, Simon, and Judas. James seems to have been Mary's second-born, and he is the same James who wrote the book of James in the New Testament.

According to the *King James Version*, *Joses* was the next son to be born, but a better translation of this name would be *Joseph*, who obviously was named after his natural father. Simon was Mary's fourth son, and he was followed by yet another who was named Judas. Interestingly, Jude is the English form of the name Judas, and it was this last half-brother of Jesus who wrote the New Testament book that bears his name.

In addition to having four brothers, Matthew 13:56 reveals Jesus also had "sisters." Since the word is plural in Greek, we know He had to have had at least two, but He could have had more. Thus, Jesus was Mary's firstborn — He was the supernaturally conceived Son of God who Joseph adopted. After Jesus was born, James, Joseph, Simon, and Jude were born, along with at least two girls. This made Mary and Joseph the parents of at least seven children.

God Loves To Call Whole Families To Be a Part of His Ministry

Now we know Jesus was the Son of God who died for the sins of the world and rose again on the third day — and that James and Jude were His half-brothers who both wrote New Testament books. What you may not know is that Mary and Joseph's other children — Joseph and Simon, as well as their daughters and their husbands — were all known to have served in ministry. This demonstrates how God loves to call entire families into His Kingdom.

We can see this principle all through the Bible, starting with the patriarchs of the Old Testament. For example, Noah and his wife along with their three sons and their wives were called as a family to fulfill God's plan to preserve a godly remnant and repopulate the earth after the flood. Likewise, Abraham and Sarah and their entire lineage were tapped by God to give birth to what would eventually be known as the nation of Israel. This included Isaac and Rebecca as well as Jacob and his 12 sons. All of them were called by God to do something impactful in the earth.

Then there was Moses, his brother Aaron, and their sister Miriam who were called by God to each play key roles in Israel's exodus from Egyptian bondage. When we cross over into the New Testament, we find Zacharias and his wife, Elisabeth, who were handpicked by God to birth and raise John the Baptist who prepared the way for Jesus' ministry. Of course we've already mentioned Mary, Joseph, and Jesus and all the other family members who were used in unprecedented ways to establish and advance God's Kingdom.

Then there were two sets of brothers — Peter and Andrew as well as James and John, the sons of Zebedee — who were selected by Jesus to serve as apostles. And we can't overlook the powerful example of the apostle Paul who was dramatically called into the ministry on the road to Damascus. What you may not know about Paul is that he had two relatives who were also called into ministry and had actually begun serving Christ *before* him. We discover this fact in Paul's letter to the believers in Rome where he says, "Salute Andronicus and Junia, my kinsmen [relatives], and my fellow-prisoners, who are of note among the apostles, who also were in Christ before me" (Romans 16:7). Imagine that! Three members of Paul's family were called into the ministry, and all of them were apostles.

The list of families being called into ministry also includes the family of Barnabas. He was a rich man who sold some of his land and gave all the proceeds to help the Church, and then God called him into the ministry (*see* Acts 4:36,37 and Acts 13). A careful reading of the Scripture reveals that he had a sister whose name was Mary, and she owned a very large apartment near the temple complex in downtown Jerusalem. It was in that apartment that Jesus and his disciples regularly met, shared the last supper, and where the Day of Pentecost took place.

This same Mary — Barnabas' sister — was the mother of a young man named John Mark. When Barnabas and Paul went on their first missionary journey, John Mark was called into the ministry and traveled with them. Later in life, John Mark became the personal assistant to the apostle Peter and actually penned what we know to be the gospel of Mark. As Peter dictated his eyewitness account of Jesus' life and ministry, Mark wrote it down, and since Mark wrote it, it's called the gospel of Mark.

Flash forward to today, and we see Rick and Denise Renner and their three sons and their wives all serving together in ministry. What's interesting is that on both Rick's side and Denise's side of the family, there were many people who were active followers of Jesus. Rick's great grandmother, who ran in the 1889 Oklahoma Land Rush on horseback, was a born-again believer who was baptized in the Holy Spirit before the Azusa Street and Topeka, Kansas outpourings ever took place. She prayed for numerous people while living in her tent on the Great Plains. For generations and generations, many individuals in the Renner lineage were saved and called into ministry.

These are just a few examples of whole families that God has saved and called into ministry, which confirms His powerful promise in Acts 16:31. It says, "…Believe on the Lord Jesus Christ, and thou shalt be saved, and thy house." Although this verse isn't a guarantee that if you get saved, the rest of your family will automatically get saved, nevertheless, it *is* a promise that something happens when you get saved and then call on the Lord on behalf of your family. As you pray for their salvation, one by one they will begin to surrender their lives to the Lord and be birthed into the family of God.

Jude Was a 'Servant' of Christ

Looking at the very first verse in Jude, he opens his letter by saying, "Jude, the servant of Jesus Christ…" (Jude 1). Isn't that interesting — he doesn't say, "This is Jude, the illustrious half-brother of Jesus." Instead, he identifies himself as "Jude, the *servant* of Jesus Christ…" (Jude 1). In Greek, there are three different words for *servant* used in the New Testament.

The first word for "servant" is *diakonos*. We find this term used in the book of Acts and is often translated as the word *deacon*. It describes *a high-level, top-notch servant that professionally serves.*

The second word for "servant" is *huperetes*. We see this word used in First Corinthians 4:1 where it is translated as the word "ministers." The apostle Paul encouraged the believers at Corinth to think of him and his co-ministers as the *huperetes*, or *servants*, of Christ. This word *huperetes* literally means *under-rowers* and was used to describe criminals who were condemned to live out the rest of their lives at the bottom of a huge ship. Their job was to take the oars that were placed in their hands and keep the ship moving forward. By using this word *huperetes*, Paul was saying, "I and all those called into ministry are like *under-rowers*. It's our job to keep the

Church moving forward and making progress. That is our life-assignment from God. If we don't row, the Church won't grow and move forward."

The third word for "servant" is *doulos*. This is what Jude called himself at the opening of his letter. This word *doulos* — translated in Jude 1 as "servant" — is *the most abject term for a slave*. It depicts *one who is totally sold into slavery and who is a slave for life*. It is *one bound to do the bidding of his owner and whose reason for existence is to help, assist, and fulfill his master's wants and dreams to the exclusion of all else*. A *doulos* is a servant who lives to serve in whatever way the master asks or demands. Hence, it is a person whose will is completely swallowed up in the will of his master.

Again, *doulos* is the word Jude used to describe himself. It is the equivalent of him saying, "I am completely surrendered and committed to Jesus, and my life is sold out to Him. My sole reason for existence now is to serve Him and do anything He asks me to do. My goal is to faithfully execute any assignment He gives to me. My will is swallowed up in His will." This type of servant attitude should be our goal as believers.

Now some may say, "We are not servants; we are sons and daughters of God." Yes, that is true. Once we're saved, God adopts us into His family, and we become His sons and daughters (*see* Romans 8:14-16; 1 John 3:1). That is our spiritual position. However, our *attitude* and *function* is that of a servant. Like Jude, we are to fully give our lives to serve the Lord. We are to listen and hear what He's saying to us and obediently do what He asks.

Jude Was a 'Brother' of James

After telling us he was a "servant of Jesus Christ," Jude added that he was a "brother of James" (Jude 1). The word "brother" here is the Greek word *adelphos*, which is derived from the old word *delphos*, the term used to describe *the womb of a woman*. When the letter "a" is placed in front of it, the word becomes *adelphos*, and it describes *two or more who were born from the same womb*.

Jude and James were brothers who were born from the womb of Mary. This was the same James who was the author of the book of James and who became the leader of the church in Jerusalem. Jude and James were the half-brothers of Jesus. Likewise, they were also spiritual brothers who were born into God's family. This endearing term was used to denote *those of one's own family* and included believers who were related spiritually, having been born out of the womb of God.

Thus, Jude opened his letter and addressed his readers by saying:

> **Jude, the servant of Jesus Christ, and brother of James, to them that are sanctified by God the Father, and preserved in Jesus Christ, and called.**
>
> —Jude 1

We Are Deeply Embedded in Christ and Greatly Loved by the Father

Now when you read this verse in the original Greek text, it is surprisingly different in a few places. For example, rather than say, "…To them that are sanctified by God the Father," it says, "…To them that are *in* God the Father," and the word "in" is a little preposition that means *to be inside of something*. In fact, you're so tucked away that you're *deeply embedded inside of it*. This is how Jude is describing our condition in Christ. The moment we repent of our sin and invite Jesus to be our Lord, we are deeply embedded inside of Him. It is the most secure place we can ever be.

Another difference between the *King James Version* and the original Greek is that instead of saying we are "sanctified by God the Father," the original text says we "have been *loved* by God the Father." So not only are you deeply embedded inside Jesus Christ, but you are also deeply *loved* by God the Father, and the word for "loved" here is a form of the Greek word *agape*, which is one of the most difficult terms in the entire New Testament to translate because it has so much meaning.

This word *agape* — translated here as "sanctified/loved" — describes *a divine love that gives, even if it's never responded to, thanked, or acknowledged*. It is a love that causes a viewer *to behold an object or person in esteem, awe, admiration, wonder, and appreciation and awakens such great respect in the heart of the observer for the object or person being beheld that he is compelled to love it*. Additionally, the word *agape* depicts *a love for a person or object that is irresistible and so profound that it knows no limits or boundaries in how far, wide, high, and deep it will go to show that love to its recipient*. It is *a self-sacrificial love that moves the lover to action*.

One of the best examples of *agape* love is when a newborn baby comes into the world and the parent sees that precious baby for the first time. They are overwhelmed with love. Even though that baby has nothing to give at that moment and can't say, "Hello Dad," or "Hello Mom," the instant his parents lay eyes on their child for the first time, they sense the surging power of *agape*. They are in awe and filled with wonder and compelled to love and sacrificially care for the child in any way they can.

This word *agape* is the same kind of love that moved God to send us Jesus. John 3:16 says, "For God so loved (*agaped*) the world, that he gave his only begotten Son, that whosoever believeth in him should not perish, but have everlasting life." When God looked at mankind and saw how we were enslaved to sin in Satan's slave market, He was moved with compassion to do something to change our condition. Compelled by His great love (*agape*), He sent Jesus to pay the price for our sin and set us free from sin's power. For all those who choose to accept His love, He embraces and places deeply inside Jesus, His Son Himself.

In our next lesson, we will look at what it means to be "preserved in Jesus Christ."

STUDY QUESTIONS

> **Study to shew thyself approved unto God, a workman that needeth not to be ashamed, rightly dividing the word of truth.**
> **— 2 Timothy 2:15**

1. Prior to this lesson, what did you know about Jude? What new details did you learn about his life, his family members, and his biological relationship to Jesus?
2. In the original Greek, Jude 1 informs us that we "...are *in* God the Father, and preserved in Jesus Christ...." This is the safest and most secure place we could ever be. How does Colossians 3:1 and Jesus' words in John 10:28-30 show you just how safe you are in your Heavenly Dad's hands?
3. Jude also tells us that we "have been *loved* by God the Father" (Jude 1). According to Romans 5:6-8 and First John 4:9 and 10, how has God demonstrated His great love for YOU?

PRACTICAL APPLICATION

> **But be ye doers of the word, and not hearers only, deceiving your own selves.**
> **—James 1:22**

1. God loves to call whole families into His Kingdom, and the Bible is full of examples. What family in Scripture stands out to you as making a great impact for God? What inspires you most about them? How does Acts 16:31 encourage you to pray, believe and watch for your unsaved family members to come to know Jesus?
2. Jude said that he was Jesus' "servant" (*doulos*), which is the equivalent of him saying, "I am completely surrendered and committed to Jesus. My sole reason for existence is to serve Him and do anything He asks me to do. My will is swallowed up in His will." Do you see yourself as Jesus' servant in this way? How did Jesus Himself model this mindset in His relationship with the Father, and what can you learn from His example? (Consider Philippians 2:5-8; Hebrews 12:2,3.)

LESSON 2

TOPIC

Experiencing the Mercy, Peace, and Love of God

SCRIPTURES

1. **Jude 1,2** — Jude, the servant of Jesus Christ, and brother of James, to them that are sanctified [loved] by God the Father, and preserved [kept] in Jesus Christ, and called: Mercy unto you, and peace, and love, be multiplied.

GREEK WORDS

1. "servant" — δοῦλος (*doulos*): the most abject term for a slave; depicts one who is totally sold into slavery and who is a slave for life; one bound to do the bidding of his owner and whose reason for existence is to help, assist, and fulfill his master's wants and dreams to the exclusion of all else; a servant who lives to serve in whatever way the master asks or demands, hence, one whose will is completely swallowed up in the will of his master
2. "brother" — ἀδελφός (*adelphos*): two or more who were born from the same womb; popularized at the time of Alexander the Great in

a military sense to depict comrades in battle; used here to describe Jude's natural-born relationship to James, who was the author of the epistle of James and was the leader of the church in Jerusalem; James and Jude were also the half-brothers of Jesus

3. "sanctified"/"loved" — ἀγάπη (*agape*): a divine love that gives, even if it's never responded to, thanked, or acknowledged; a love that causes a viewer to behold an object or person in esteem, awe, admiration, wonder, and appreciation and awakens such great respect in the heart of the observer for the object or person being beheld that he is compelled to love it; a love for a person or object that is irresistible and so profound that it knows no limits or boundaries in how far, wide, high, and deep it will go to show that love to its recipient; a self-sacrificial love that moves the lover to action

4. "kept" — τηρέω (*tereo*): used in literature to depict the uninterrupted vigilance of soldiers who were positioned to protect something of great importance; used to describe the uninterrupted vigilance of shepherds who were charged to watch over the sheep assigned to their watch; soldiers charged to stand guard who knew they were to be faithful and to remain committed to their charge regardless of assaults or the number of attackers they might encounter; Jude used this word to depict Christ as One who stands attentively on guard over each of us

5. "called" — κλητός (*kletos*): to beckon, call, invite, or summon; often used to convey the idea of those called or invited to an event that was normally closed to the public, thus, an event that one could only participate in by a VIP invitation; the word κλητός (*kletos*) was used to describe a special invitation extended by a king who asked people to attend a feast; because such royal events were closed to the public, a person couldn't attend without being invited, thus, receiving an invitation to attend this type of special occasion was considered an honor to be treasured, prized, and revered

6. "mercy" — ἔλεος (*eleos*): pity, compassion, or the deep-seated and unsettling emotions a person feels in response to something he has seen or heard; a deep-seated emotion that compels one to action

7. "peace" — εἰρήνη (*eirene*): the cessation of war; an end of conflict; a time of rebuilding and reconstructing after war has ceased; distractions removed; a time of prosperity; the rule of order in place of chaos; a calm, inner stability that results in the ability to conduct oneself peacefully even in the midst of circumstances that would normally be traumatic or upsetting; the Greek equivalent for the Hebrew word

"shalom," which expresses the idea of wholeness, completeness, or tranquility in the soul that is unaffected by outward circumstances or pressures

8. "love" — ἀγάπη (*agape*): a divine love that gives, even if it's never responded to, thanked, or acknowledged; a love that causes a viewer to behold an object or person in esteem, awe, admiration, wonder, and appreciation and awakens such great respect in the heart of the observer for the object or person being beheld that he is compelled to love it; a love for a person or object that is irresistible and so profound that it knows no limits or boundaries in how far, wide, high, and deep it will go to show that love to its recipient; a self-sacrificial love that moves the lover to action

9. "multiplied" — πληθύνω (*plethuno*): to amplify, to make full, to increase, to maximize, or to multiply; something that is rapidly escalating in terms of quality, quantity, and size; something becoming fuller and more bountiful

SYNOPSIS

As we noted in Lesson 1, the name Jude is the English equivalent of the name Judas, which you probably remember was the name of the man who scandalously betrayed Jesus into the hands of the Jewish rulers. In contrast to Judas Iscariot, this Jude was a totally devoted servant of Jesus and an ardent defender of the Christian faith, which is the focus of his brief book made up of only 25 verses.

The emphasis of this lesson:

Moved by His immense mercy and love, God has given us a VIP invitation into His salvation. This is a tremendous honor to be treasured, prized, and revered. Jude prayed for all believers to experience God's supernatural mercy, love, and peace and that it would be multiplied — amplified, made full, and maximized — in our lives.

A REVIEW OF LESSON 1
Jude Was Jesus' Half-Brother

Jude was the half-brother of Jesus. He and Jesus had the same mother — Mary — but they had different fathers. When Mary was engaged to be married to Joseph — *before* they came together sexually — she became pregnant when the Holy Spirit came upon her and supernaturally conceived Jesus (*see* Luke 1:35). Thus, Jesus was her firstborn son — the Son of God Himself.

After Jesus birth, time passed and Mary and Joseph came together and produced several children, including James, Joses (Joseph), Simon, and Judas (Jude) (*see* Matthew 13:55). It is understood that James was Mary's second-born, and he became the leader of the church in Jerusalem and is the same James who wrote the book of James in the New Testament.

Joses — or Joseph — was the next son to be born, who was obviously named after his father, and Mary and Joseph's fourth son was Simon. Jude was their fifth son, and he is the one who wrote the New Testament book that bears his name.

According to Matthew 13:56, Jesus also had "sisters." Since the word is plural in Greek, we know He had to have had at least two, but He could have had more. Thus, when we look at Mary and Joseph's family, we see Jesus — Mary's firstborn — the supernaturally conceived Son of God. And after Jesus, there came James, Joseph, Simon, and Jude, along with at least two girls. This made Mary and Joseph the parents of at least seven children.

This entire family was called by God into the ministry. We know that Jesus was God in the flesh who died for the sins of the world and rose again on the third day. James and Jude were His half-brothers who eventually became leaders in the Church and wrote New Testament books. Moreover, early Christian writers tell us Mary and Joseph's other children — Joseph and Simon, as well as their daughters and their husbands — were all known to have served in ministry. This demonstrates how God delights in calling entire families into His Kingdom.

Jude Was Jesus' 'Servant'

It's interesting to note that Jude identified himself as "…the servant of Jesus Christ, and brother of James…" (Jude 1). The word "brother" here is the Greek word *adelphos*, which describes *two or more who were born from the same womb*. The fact that Jude used this word confirms that he and James were natural-born brothers. They were also both Jesus' half-brother, but rather than focus on the fact, Jude called himself Jesus' *servant*.

As we saw in Lesson 1, there are three primary words for "servant" in the New Testament.

The first word for "servant" is *diakonos*, and it's where we get the word *deacon*. We find this term used in Acts 6, and it describes *a high-level, top-notch servant that professionally serves*.

The second word for "servant" is *huperetes*. We see the apostle Paul use this term in First Corinthians 4:1 where he encourages the believers at Corinth to think of him and those serving alongside him as "ministers of Christ." The word "ministers" here is *huperetes*, and it literally means *under-rowers*. This word was used to describe criminals who were condemned to live out the rest of their lives at the bottom of ship galleys. After being chained to a bench and an oar being placed in their hands, it was their job to listen to the captain above and keep rowing to maintain the ship's forward motion.

By using this word *huperetes*, Paul was saying, "I and all those called into ministry are like *under-rowers*. It's our job to keep the Church moving forward and making progress. That's our life-assignment from God. If we don't row, the Church won't grow and move forward." The truth is if you're serving in an area of ministry, you, too, are an under-rower. Whether you're a deacon, an elder, a nursery worker, youth sponsor, Sunday school teacher, or worship-team member, it's your job to get in position, grab your spiritual oars, and do what God has called you to do to keep the church moving forward.

The third word for "servant" is *doulos*. When Jude identified himself as Jesus' "servant," he used the word *doulos*, which is *the most abject term for a slave*. It depicts *one who is totally sold into slavery and who is a slave for life*. It is *one bound to do the bidding of his owner and whose reason for existence is to help, assist, and fulfill his master's wants and dreams to the exclusion of all* else. A *doulos* is one whose will is completely swallowed up in the will of his master.

This is the word Jude used to describe himself. It was the equivalent of him saying, "I am sold-out to do the will of Jesus. I'll do whatever He asks me to do and go wherever He asks me to go. My job is to faithfully carry out every assignment He gives me. My will is swallowed up in His will." This type of servant attitude should be our goal as believers.

Now some people may say, "I thought we were sons and daughters of God. Is that not true?" Yes, we are sons and daughters of God if we're born again. That is our privileged position according to First John 3:1 and 2. God has adopted us into His family and calls us His very own (*see* Romans 8:15 and 23; Ephesians 1:4-6). Yet, our attitude and function is to be that of a servant (*doulos*). We are to be willing to do anything God asks us to do, and our will is to be swallowed up in His will.

We Are Greatly Loved by God and Permanently Placed in Christ

After Jude tells us he is the brother of James and servant of Jesus Christ, he continues by saying, "…To them that are sanctified by God the Father, and preserved in Jesus Christ, and called: Mercy unto you, and peace, and love, be multiplied" (Jude 1,2).

As we saw in Lesson 1, the original Greek text of this passage doesn't say, "…To them that are sanctified by God the Father." Instead, it says, "…To them that are *in* God the Father," and the word "in" is a preposition, which means *in*, *inside*, or *located inside of*. It gives the impression of one that is permanently located in the interior of a particular sphere and who operates inside the sphere where he has been permanently located. In this case, Jude is describing us being *inside Christ, deeply embedded in Him*, and in Christ, the enemy cannot touch us. As believers, Christ is our new spiritual location, and we must make it our aim for this truth to become our experiential reality.

The original Greek here also adds that we "…have been *loved* by God the Father," and the word for "loved" here is a form of the Greek word *agape*, which describes *a love so profound it knows no limits*. This is the same love described in John 3:16, where Jesus said, "For God so loved (*agaped*) the world, that he gave his only begotten Son, that whosoever believeth in him should not perish, but have everlasting life." When God looked at humanity, He saw past our faults and failures and was able to see us freed from Satan's control and alive in Christ. Moved by love (*agape*), He sent us Jesus to pay the price for our sin and set us free from sin's power.

That's what *agape* (love) is — *a divine love that gives, even if it's never responded to, thanked, or acknowledged*. It is a love that causes a viewer *to behold an object or person in esteem, awe, admiration, wonder, and appreciation* and awakens such great respect in the heart of the observer for the object or person being beheld that he is compelled to love it. God's *agape* (love) for us is so profound that it knows no limits or boundaries in how far, wide, high, and deep it will go to show that love.

We Are 'Preserved' in Jesus

In addition to being loved by God and embedded in Christ, Jude also said we are "preserved in Jesus" (Jude 1). In Greek, the word "preserved" is a form of the word *tereo*, which means *to keep, to guard*, or *to protect*. It was used in literature to depict *the uninterrupted vigilance of soldiers who were positioned to protect something of great importance*. Likewise, it was also employed to describe *the uninterrupted vigilance of shepherds who were charged to guard the sheep assigned to their watch*. It didn't matter if wolves, bears, lions, or any other predators came to attack the sheep. The shepherd's assignment was to preserve (*tereo*) his flock.

Jude used this word to depict Christ as the One who stands attentively on guard over each of us. Once we're embedded deeply inside of Him, we become His responsibility. Like a trustworthy soldier charged to faithfully stand guard and fulfill his charge regardless of assaults or the number of attackers he might encounter, Christ watches over us. We are the members of His flock.

We Are 'Called' by Jesus

Along with being preserved in Jesus, Jude goes on to say that we are also "called" (*see* Jude 1). This word "called" is a form of the Greek word *kletos*, which means *to beckon, call, invite, or summon*. It was often used to convey the idea of *those called or invited to an event that was normally closed to the public — an event that one could only participate in by a VIP invitation*. Furthermore, this word *kletos* was used to describe *a special invitation extended by a king who asked people to attend a feast*, and because such royal events were closed to the public, a person couldn't attend without being invited. Thus, receiving an invitation to attend this type of special occasion was considered an honor to be treasured, prized, and revered.

Here we see Jude using this word *kletos* — translated as "called" — to let us know that we could have never come to Christ by ourselves. God had to invite us into salvation. He gave us a VIP invitation, which we should consider a tremendous honor to be *treasured*, *prized*, and *revered*. This truth is confirmed by Jesus Himself who said, "No man can come to me, except the Father which hath sent me draw him…" (John 6:44). Indeed, before coming to Jesus, we were all dead in our sins — unable to see or hear the Gospel (*see* Ephesians 2:1). It was God's great mercy and love that made a way for us to be back in relationship with Him.

Mercy, Peace, and Love Be Multiplied to You

When we come to the second verse of Jude's letter, he speaks a blessing upon all his readers, saying, "Mercy unto you, and peace, and love, be multiplied" (Jude 2). First, notice the word "mercy" — the Greek word *eleos*. It can be translated as *pity*, *compassion*, or *the deep-seated and unsettling emotions a person feels in response to something he has seen or heard*. But *eleos* is more than just feeling bad about what has happened to someone. It is *a deep-seated emotion of compassion that compels one to action*.

For example, maybe you see a child who is homeless or has no food. Rather than just stand by and say, "Oh, that's just so sad," you are so moved by what you see and hear that you decide right then and there to do something to change that child's dire situation. That's what the word "mercy" (*eleos*) means in this verse. Thus, Jude is saying, "I'm praying for God to extend *mercy* to you so powerfully that it will totally change your situation."

The next thing Jude prays for his readers to receive is "peace," which in Greek is the word *eirene*. It describes *the cessation of war* and pictures *an end of conflict* and *a time of rebuilding and reconstructing after war has ceased*. This peace means distractions are removed, a time of prosperity sets in, and the rule of order replaces chaos. This word *eirene* (peace) describes *a calm, inner stability that results in the ability to conduct oneself peacefully even in the midst of circumstances that would normally be traumatic or upsetting*. Moreover, the word *eirene* is the equivalent of the Hebrew word *shalom*, which expresses the idea of *wholeness*, *completeness*, or *tranquility in the soul that is unaffected by outward circumstances or pressures.* In context, Jude is praying for God' supernatural peace to be given to the believers he's writing to.

The third provision Jude asks the Father to give to his readers is "love," which once again is the Greek word *agape*. It is *a divine love that gives, even if it's never responded to, thanked, or acknowledged* — a love that causes a viewer to behold an object or person in esteem, awe, admiration, wonder, and appreciation and awakens such great respect in the heart of the observer for the object or person being beheld that he is compelled to love it.

Jude prayed that mercy, peace, and love be "multiplied" in the lives of his readers. This word "multiplied" is the Greek word *plethuno*, which means *to amplify, to make full, to increase, to maximize*, or *to multiply*. It depicts *something that is rapidly escalating in terms of quality, quantity, and size; something becoming fuller and more bountiful.*

Taking into account the original Greek meaning of all these words, here is the *Renner Interpretive Version (RIV)* of Jude 1 and 2:

> **I am Jude — first and foremost a completely sold-out, committed, lifelong servant of Jesus Christ. And as is true with all such servants, that means I live solely to do His will and to faithfully carry out any assignment He will ever entrust to me. I also am the natural-born brother of James. But in this letter, I am writing to those who are in God the Father — to those who are deeply embedded inside Him and have experienced the inexpressible, indescribable, unspeakable love of God. I'm talking about privileged people that Jesus Christ has personally extended His VIP invitation to — and having accepted that invitation, are now guarded, kept, preserved, and protected by Jesus Christ, who, like a soldier faithfully watching over an assignment, or like a shepherd who faithfully watches over his flock, He is faithfully guarding and keeping watch over each and every one who belongs to Him.**
>
> **Mercy to you — a mercy that compels God to act on your behalf, and peace to you — a peace that bring cessation to wars in your life, closure to conflicts, removes distractions, allows a time for rebuilding and reconstruction, ushers in prosperity, fosters the rule of order in the place of chaos, and a peace that produces a calm, inner stability that results in the ability to**

conduct yourself peacefully even in the midst of circumstances that would normally be traumatic or upsetting. Oh, I also wish for God's love to be multiplied in your life — that is, that this love would escalate and abundantly multiply in your life.

In our next lesson, we will continue our study in Jude and explore what he means when he issues the charge to "earnestly contend for the faith" (Jude 3).

STUDY QUESTIONS

> Study to shew thyself approved unto God, a workman that needeth not to be ashamed, rightly dividing the word of truth.
> — 2 Timothy 2:15

1. Your pastor (or pastors) may stand on a stage and seem to live in the limelight, but the truth is he or she is an under-rower of God's Kingdom. He's always on call, working tirelessly in prayer, preparing messages, and caring for people because he knows that if he doesn't do what he's called to do, your church won't move forward. According to First Thessalonians 5:12,13; First Timothy 2:1-3; and Hebrews 13:7, what does God want you to do to show your pastor your support and appreciation? (Also consider Galatians 6:10.)

2. Once we are "preserved" — embedded deeply inside — of Christ, we become His responsibility. Like a trustworthy, committed soldier or shepherd, He stands attentively on guard over each of us, faithfully protecting us against all the enemy's assaults. What are some examples of what His protection can look like in our lives? (Consider Psalm 121 and 91; Second Timothy 1:12; Jude 24.)

PRACTICAL APPLICATION

> But be ye doers of the word, and not hearers only, deceiving your own selves.
> — James 1:22

1. Jude tells us we have been "called" (*kletos*) into God's wonderful salvation. He's given us a VIP invitation to receive His forgiveness and be adopted into His family. How does knowing you could never have earned His gift of salvation help you genuinely treasure and prize God's invitation?

2. Can you remember a time when God extended mercy (*eleos*) to you — when you were in a dire situation, and He showed up to comfort you and bring you through the challenge? What happened? How did your love for Him grow through the experience?

LESSON 3

TOPIC
What It Means To Earnestly Contend for the Faith

SCRIPTURES

1. **Jude 1-3** — Jude, the servant of Jesus Christ, and brother of James, to them that are sanctified [loved] by God the Father, and preserved [kept] in Jesus Christ, and called: Mercy unto you, and peace, and love, be multiplied. Beloved, when I gave all diligence to write unto you of the common salvation, it was needful for me to write unto you, and exhort you that ye should earnestly contend for the faith which was once delivered unto the saints.

2. **2 Peter 2:1-3** — But there were false prophets also among the people, even as there shall be false teachers among you, who privily shall bring in damnable heresies, even denying the Lord that bought them, and bring upon themselves swift destruction. And many shall follow their pernicious ways; by reason of whom the way of truth shall be evil spoken of. And through covetousness shall they with feigned words make merchandise of you: whose judgment now of a long time lingereth not, and their damnation slumbereth not.

GREEK WORDS

1. "servant" — δοῦλος (*doulos*): the most abject term for a slave; depicts one who is totally sold into slavery and who is a slave for life; one bound to do the bidding of his owner and whose reason for existence is to help, assist, and fulfill his master's wants and dreams to the exclusion of all else; a servant who lives to serve in whatever way the master

asks or demands, hence, one whose will is completely swallowed up in the will of his master

2. "brother" — ἀδελφός (*adelphos*): two or more who were born from the same womb; popularized at the time of Alexander the Great in a military sense to depict comrades in battle; used here to describe Jude's natural-born relationship to James, who was the author of the epistle of James and was the leader of the church in Jerusalem; James and Jude were also the half-brothers of Jesus

3. "sanctified"/"loved" — ἀγάπη (*agape*): a divine love that gives, even if it's never responded to, thanked, or acknowledged; a love that causes a viewer to behold an object or person in esteem, awe, admiration, wonder, and appreciation and awakens such great respect in the heart of the observer for the object or person being beheld that he is compelled to love it; a love for a person or object that is irresistible and so profound that it knows no limits or boundaries in how far, wide, high, and deep it will go to show that love to its recipient; a self-sacrificial love that moves the lover to action

4. "preserved"/"kept" — τηρέω (*tereo*): used in literature to depict the uninterrupted vigilance of soldiers who were positioned to protect something of great importance; used to describe the uninterrupted vigilance of shepherds who were charged to watch over the sheep assigned to their watch; soldiers charged to stand guard who knew they were to be faithful and to remain committed to their charge regardless of assaults or the number of attackers they might encounter; Jude used this word to depict Christ as One who stands attentively on guard over each of us

5. "called" — κλητός (*kletos*): to beckon, call, invite, or summon; often used to convey the idea of those called or invited to an event that was normally closed to the public, thus, an event that one could only participate in by a VIP invitation; the word κλητός (*kletos*) was used to describe a special invitation extended by a king who asked people to attend a feast; because such royal events were closed to the public, a person couldn't attend without being invited, thus, receiving an invitation to attend this type of special occasion was considered an honor to be treasured, prized, and revered

6. "mercy" — ἔλεος (*eleos*): pity, compassion, or the deep-seated and unsettling emotions a person feels in response to something he has seen or heard; a deep-seated emotion that compels one to action

7. "peace" — εἰρήνη (*eirene*): the cessation of war; an end of conflict; a time of rebuilding and reconstructing after war has ceased; distractions removed; a time of prosperity; the rule of order in place of chaos; a calm, inner stability that results in the ability to conduct oneself peacefully even in the midst of circumstances that would normally be traumatic or upsetting; the Greek equivalent for the Hebrew word "shalom," which expresses the idea of wholeness, completeness, or tranquility in the soul that is unaffected by outward circumstances or pressures

8. "love" — ἀγάπη (*agape*): a divine love that gives, even if it's never responded to, thanked, or acknowledged; a love that causes a viewer to behold an object or person in esteem, awe, admiration, wonder, and appreciation and awakens such great respect in the heart of the observer for the object or person being beheld that he is compelled to love it; a love for a person or object that is irresistible and so profound that it knows no limits or boundaries in how far, wide, high, and deep it will go to show that love to its recipient; a self-sacrificial love that moves the lover to action

9. "multiplied" — πληθύνω (*plethuno*): to amplify, to make full, to increase, to maximize, or to multiply; something that is rapidly escalating in terms of quality, quantity, and size; something becoming fuller and more bountiful

10. "beloved" — ἀγαπητοὶ (*agapetoi*): plural version of ἀγάπη (*agape*) used to describe one's deep love for others; beloved; as with ἀγάπη (*agape*) it describes the admiration one has for an object of beauty; depicts an observer who experiences a loss of words to express what he feels because he is so taken with the beauty of an object or person; Jude used ἀγαπητοὶ (*agapetoi*) to mean we, as believers, should view one another with deep admiration, awe, and wonder

11. "diligence" — σπουδάζω (*spoudadzo*): to do something with eagerness; to do something with diligence; acting responsibly, quickly, and with attentiveness; one so diligent, excited, and energetic that he puts his whole heart into the principle or task before him; to do something with excitement, enthusiasm, and haste because it is so important, serious, or urgent; to give one's best efforts to a project or task and to do it enthusiastically; this word informs us Jude was excited about his plan to write an epistle about salvation and all of its mutually shared benefits

12. "common" — **κοινός** (*koinos*): what is commonly or mutually shared; could denote shared property or the benefits of a shared relationship; by using **κοινός** (*koinos*), Jude acknowledged that salvation has many benefits that mutually belong to all believers
13. "salvation" — **σωτηρία** (*soteria*): salvation; deliverance, healing, preservation, prosperity, safety, and general welfare
14. "needful" — **ἀνάγκη** (*anagke*): an urgent necessity
15. "exhort" — **παρακαλέω** (*parakaleo*): often used in ancient times to depict military leaders who came alongside their troops to urge, exhort, beseech, beg, and plead with them to stand tall and face their battles bravely
16. "earnestly contend" — **ἐπαγωνίζομαι** (*epagonidzomai*): a compound of **ἐπί** (*epi*) and **ἀγωνίζομαι** (*agonidzomai*); the preposition **ἐπί** (*epi*) means for or over, and it is used as an intensifier in the word **ἐπαγωνίζομαι** (*epagonidzomai*); the word **ἀγωνίζομαι** (*agonidzomai*) denotes an intense struggle and is where we derive the word "agony"; it was used to picture two wrestlers who agonized to win over the other in a wrestling match; both wrestlers worked to gain the advantage and hurl their opponent to the ground, exerting every ounce of their strength and skill to win a very intense physical contest; when **ἐπί** (*epi*) and **ἀγωνίζομαι** (*agonidzomai*) are compounded into a single word, it depicts those who are fighting with all of their might to win a match of some type, agonizing over it; Jude's use of this word means he was urging his readers to intensely fight over an issue or to fight for a truth
17. "once" — **ἅπαξ** (*hapax*): completion, finality, or something so complete that it needs nothing more to be added to it
18. "delivered" — **παραδίδωμι** (*paradidomi*): a compound of the preposition **παρα** (*para*) and **δίδωμι** (*didomi*); **παρα** (*para*) means along, as to pass something from one to the other, and the word **δίδωμι** (*didomi*) means to hand over, to pass to another, to transmit, or to transfer; in this verse, it means to deliver over to someone or to entrust to someone for their safekeeping, for example, as one would pass a tradition from one generation to another

SYNOPSIS

For a carpenter, easily the most important tool he uses in every project is his tape measure. It is his standard of measurement that never changes and provides accuracy for cutting, alignment, and positioning in everything he builds. As believers, the Word of God is our spiritual tape measure—it provides unchanging accuracy to help us build our lives and stand up for truth. In order to be able to "earnestly contend for the faith" as Jude urges, we have to *know* the Word and be *in* the Word. Handling truth consistently is the best way to recognize and reject the enemy's attempts to deceive us.

The emphasis of this lesson:

Jude was excited and enthusiastic to write about all the mutual benefits our salvation entails, but after reading Peter's second letter about false prophets invading the Church, he felt compelled to expand on what Peter had written and urge his readers to earnestly contend for the faith.

A REVIEW OF LESSONS 1 AND 2

Jude Was a Sold-Out Servant of Jesus and the Natural-Born Brother of James

Jude opens his letter by saying, "Jude, the servant of Jesus Christ, and brother of James, to them that are sanctified by God the Father, and preserved in Jesus Christ, and called" (Jude 1). So far we have seen that the writer of this book is none other than Jude, the half-brother of Jesus. Both Jude and Jesus had the same mother — Mary — but different fathers. Jude's father was Joseph, and Jesus' Father was God.

Although Jude could have built up his reputation by announcing that he was the distinguished half-brother of Jesus, he didn't. Instead, he called himself the "servant of Jesus Christ," and the word "servant" here is *doulos*, which is *the most abject term for a slave* in the New Testament. This word depicts *one bound to do the bidding of his owner and whose reason for existence is to help, assist, and fulfill his master's wants and dreams to the exclusion of all else*. Hence, Jude is telling his readers, "I'm sold-out lock, stock, and barrel to exclusively do whatever Jesus asks of me. My job is to faithfully carry out any assignment He gives me. My will is completely swallowed up in His will."

The same mindset that Jude had we need to have too. Yes, we are the sons and daughters of God, and what a privilege it is to call Him "Abba

Father." Nevertheless, in our attitude and practice, we are to be the Lord's servants and be ready to do anything Jesus asks us to do. Our will is to be swallowed up in His will, and our existence is to help, assist, and fulfill whatever *His* wants and dreams are to the exclusion of all else.

In addition to being the half-brother of Jesus, Jude was also the "brother of James" (Jude 1). We have noted that the word "brother" is the Greek word *adelphos*, which describes *two or more who were born from the same womb*. This word was popularized at the time of Alexander the Great in a military sense to depict *comrades in battle*. Here it is used to describe Jude's natural-born relationship to James, who was the writer of the book of James and the leader of the church in Jerusalem. James and Jude were both the half-brothers of Jesus.

You Are Embedded in God and Greatly Loved by Him

In his next breath, Jude gives us a picture of our position and condition as believers when he says, "…To them that are sanctified by God the Father, and preserved in Jesus Christ, and called" (Jude 1). As we have noted, when we read this verse in the Greek, it actually says, "…To them that are *in* God the Father…," and the word "in" is the preposition *en*, which means *in, inside,* or *located inside of*. It depicts *one that is deeply and permanently embedded in God* — a place where the enemy cannot touch us.

The original Greek here also adds that we "…have been *loved* by God the Father," and the word "loved" is a form of the Greek word *agape*, which describes *a divine love that gives, even if it's never responded to, thanked, or acknowledged*. It is *a love that causes a viewer to behold an object or person in esteem, awe, admiration, wonder, and appreciation* and awakens such great respect in the heart of the observer for the object or person being beheld that he is compelled to love it and do something for it.

It's this same kind of love — *agape* — that is celebrated in John 3:16, which says, "For God so loved the world, that he gave his only begotten Son, that whosoever believeth in him should not perish, but have everlasting life." When God looked at all the people of the world, He was filled with such awe and admiration inside His heart that He couldn't just feel sad and pity us. Instead, His love ignited a compelling desire to get personally involved and do something to change our situation. Jude reminds us of this inexpressible love that is ours in Him. God's love — *agape* — for us is so profound that it knows no limits or boundaries in how far, wide, high, and deep it will go to show that love.

You Are Guarded and Protected in Jesus and Given a VIP Invitation to His Salvation

Along with being intensely loved, Jude says we are also "…preserved in Jesus Christ, and called" (Jude 1). The word "preserved" here is a form of the Greek word *tereo*, which means *to be guarded, kept, preserved*, and *protected*. It denoted the uninterrupted vigilance of soldiers who were assigned to protect something of great importance, such as property. The word *tereo* was also used to describe the uninterrupted vigilance of shepherds who were charged to watch over the sheep assigned to their watch. They were committed to keep their eyes on their flock and remain faithful to their assignment regardless of assaults or the number of attackers they might encounter. Jude used this word *tereo* to describe how Jesus stands attentively on guard over each of us.

This brings us to the word "called," which is a form of the Greek word *kletos*, and it means *to beckon, call, invite*, or *summon*. It was often used to convey the idea of those called or invited to an event that was normally closed to the public. The use of the word *kletos* tells us that if you are a child of God, Jesus has extended a VIP invitation to you to join in His salvation. You could never have come to Him on your own, which Jesus confirms in John 6:44 and 14:6. This special invitation extended by the King of kings is to be considered a prestigious honor to be treasured, prized, and revered.

Taking into account the original Greek meaning of all these words, here is the *Renner Interpretive Version (RIV)* of Jude 1:

> **I am Jude — first and foremost a completely sold-out, committed, lifelong servant of Jesus Christ. And as is true with all such servants, that means I live solely to do His will and to faithfully carry out any assignment He will ever entrust to me. I also am the natural-born brother of James. But in this letter, I am writing to those who are in God the Father — to those who are deeply embedded inside Him and have experienced the inexpressible, indescribable, unspeakable love of God. I'm talking about privileged people that Jesus Christ has personally extended His VIP invitation to — and having accepted that**

invitation, are now guarded, kept, preserved, and protected by Jesus Christ, who, like a soldier faithfully watching over an assignment, or like a shepherd who faithfully watches over his flock, He is faithfully guarding and keeping watch over each and every one who belongs to Him.

Jude Declared God's Blessings of Mercy, Peace, and Love on Us

In verse 2 of Jude's letter, he declared a blessing on all his hearers, saying, "Mercy unto you, and peace, and love, be multiplied" (Jude 2). We saw in our previous lesson that the word "mercy" is the Greek word *eleos*, which can be translated as *pity* or *compassion*, only in this case it is more than just a fleeting feeling of sadness over what has happened to someone. This word *eleos* is *a deep-seated compassion that compels one to action*. Rather than just wring our hands and say, "Oh, that's just so sad," mercy drives us to step in and do something to change a person's situation. Here, Jude is praying that God will extend His mercy to us by personally stepping in and changing our situation.

Jude also prayed for us to receive "peace." In Greek, this is the word *eirene*, and it describes *the cessation of war* and *the end of conflict*. It denotes *a time of rebuilding and reconstructing after war has ceased*. Distractions have been removed, and a time of prosperity has set in. This word *eirene* (peace) describes *a calm, inner stability that results in the ability to conduct oneself peacefully even in the midst of circumstances that would normally be traumatic or upsetting*. Interestingly, the word *eirene* is the equivalent of the Hebrew word *shalom*, which expresses the idea of *wholeness, completeness*, or *tranquility in the soul*. Here, Jude is praying for God's supernatural peace to be given to the believers he's writing to — including us.

There's one more virtue Jude asked the Father to give us and that is "love." Again, this is the Greek word *agape*, and it describes the inexpressible, indescribable marvelous love of God. It is *a divine love that gives, even if it's never responded to, thanked, or acknowledged*. Jude prayed that love, mercy, and peace would be "multiplied" in our lives. The word "multiplied" is the Greek word *plethuno*, which means *to amplify, to make full, to increase, to maximize*, or *to multiply*. It depicts *something that is rapidly escalating in terms of quality, quantity, and size*.

Taking into account the original Greek meaning of all these words, here is the *Renner Interpretive Version (RIV)* of Jude 2:

> **Mercy to you** — a mercy that compels God to act on your behalf, **and peace to you** — a peace that brings cessation to wars in your life, closure to conflicts, removes distractions, allows a time for rebuilding and reconstruction, ushers in prosperity, fosters the rule of order in the place of chaos, and a peace that produces a calm, inner stability that results in the ability to conduct yourself peacefully even in the midst of circumstances that would normally be traumatic or upsetting. Oh, I also wish for God's love to be multiplied in your life — that is, that this love would escalate and abundantly multiply in your life.

Jude Intended To Write About Our Shared Benefits of Salvation

After Jude's opening words, he states his purpose for writing by saying, "Beloved, when I gave all diligence to write unto you of the common salvation, it was needful for me to write unto you, and exhort you that ye should earnestly contend for the faith which was once delivered unto the saints" (Jude 3). This passage is bursting with truth, so let's begin unpacking some of the key words, starting with the word "beloved."

In Greek, "beloved" is the word *agapetoi*, which is the plural version of *agape*. It is used to describe *one's deep love for others*, and as with *agape*, it describes *the admiration one has for an object of beauty*. Moreover, it depicts *an observer who experiences a loss of words to express what he feels because he is so taken with the beauty of an object or person*. Here, Jude uses the term *agapetoi* — translated as "beloved" — to say that we, as believers, should view one another with deep admiration, awe, and wonder.

When Jude said, "…I gave all diligence to write unto you…" (Jude 3), the word "diligence" is a form of the Greek word *spoudadzo*, which means *to do something with eagerness or diligence*. It denotes *acting responsibly, quickly, and with attentiveness*. It is the picture of *one so diligent, excited, and energetic that he puts his whole heart into the principle or task before him*. This word *spoudadzo* signifies *doing something with excitement, enthusiasm, and haste because it is so important, serious, or urgent*. It means *to give one's best efforts to a project or task and to do it enthusiastically*. Jude's use of this word informs us that he was excited about his plan to write an epistle about salvation and all of its mutually shared benefits.

This brings us to the word "common" — the Greek word *koinos*. It describes *what is commonly or mutually shared* and can denote *shared property* or *the benefits of a shared relationship such as that of a husband and wife*. In this case, Jude wanted to write about and discuss the many benefits of "salvation" that mutually belong to all believers. In Greek, the word "salvation" is a form of the word *soteria*, and it describes *salvation, deliverance, healing, preservation, prosperity, safety, and general welfare*. It was all these amazing benefits that Jude was so eager (*spoudadzo*) to discuss.

Peter's Second Letter Powerfully Influenced Jude

As Jude was about to talk about all that is ours through the shed blood of Jesus, something happened that redirected his attention. In fact, he said, "…It was needful for me to write unto you, and exhort you that ye should earnestly contend for the faith which was once delivered unto the saints" (Jude 3). The word "needful" is a translation of the Greek word *anagke*, which denotes *an urgent necessity*. What was it that was so urgent that caused Jude to abandon his plans to write about salvation?

It appears that he came across Peter's second letter to believers, and it so impacted him that he felt compelled to expand on what Peter had written. What did Jude read that arrested his attention? Peter said:

> **But there were false prophets also among the people, even as there shall be false teachers among you, who privily shall bring in damnable heresies, even denying the Lord that bought them, and bring upon themselves swift destruction.**
>
> **And many shall follow their pernicious ways; by reason of whom the way of truth shall be evil spoken of.**
>
> **And through covetousness shall they with feigned words make merchandise of you: whose judgment now of a long time lingereth not, and their damnation slumbereth not.**
> **— 2 Peter 2:1-3**

If you read further into Peter's letter, he goes on to talk about these corrupt men who stealthily snuck into the Church and began to deceive and take advantage of the people through their false doctrines. These words were so alarming to Jude that he felt it was needed (*anagke*) to scrap his original writing plans and exhort his readers to earnestly contend for the faith.

The word "exhort" in Jude 3 is a form of the familiar Greek word *parakaleo*, a term often used in ancient times to depict military leaders who came alongside their troops to urge, exhort, beseech, beg, and plead with them to stand tall and face their battles bravely. The fact that Jude used this word *parakaleo* means that he saw himself as a general in the faith who needed to strengthen the troops by telling them it was time to "…earnestly contend for the faith which was once delivered unto the saints" (Jude 3).

Jude Charged His Readers To 'Earnestly Contend for the Faith'

The phrase "earnestly contend" is a translation of the Greek word *epagonidzomai*, which is a compound of the words *epi* and *agonidzomai*. The word *epi* is a preposition meaning *for* or *over* that is an intensifier of the word *agonidzomai*, which denotes *an intense struggle* and is where we derive the word "agony." It is actually a picture of two wrestlers who agonized to win over the other in a wrestling match; both wrestlers worked to gain the advantage and hurl their opponent to the ground, exerting every ounce of their strength and skill to win a very intense physical contest.

When *epi* and *agonidzomai* are compounded to form *epagonidzomai*, it means *to earnestly agonize over something*. It depicts *those who are fighting with all of their might to win a match of some type, agonizing over it*. In this case, Jude's use of this word means he was urging his readers to intensely fight over or to fight for truth "…which was once delivered unto the saints" (Jude 3).

The word "once" in Greek is *hapax*, and it describes *completion, finality*, or *something so complete that it needs nothing more to be added to it*. And the word "delivered" is a form of the Greek *paradidomi*, which is a compound of the preposition *para* and the word *didomi*. The word *para* means *along*, as to pass something from one to the other; and the word *didomi* means *to hand over, to pass to another, to transmit*, or *to transfer*. When these words come together to form *paradidomi*, it means *to deliver over to someone or to entrust to someone for their safekeeping.* An example would be the passing of a tradition from one generation to another.

Taking into account the original Greek meaning of all these words, here is the *Renner Interpretive Version (RIV)* of this part of Jude 3:

> **Beloved — I call you that because it's the only word I know to express how deeply I love and cherish you — I fully intended to write to you about our mutually shared salvation, and I was eager to write about this exciting subject, ready to engage all my creative abilities to dive deep into all the benefits that our salvation entails. But as I was about to get started, I found myself gripped with a sense of urgency and a deeply felt need to address another subject that came to my attention. I felt someone needed to come alongside the troops — to urge them to hold their head high, to throw their shoulders back and, if needed, to look the enemy eyeball to eyeball and to earnestly contend for the faith because it is under assault….**

In our next lesson, we will uncover the meaning of the remainder of Jude 3 and explore what God is telling us in verse 4.

STUDY QUESTIONS

> Study to shew thyself approved unto God, a workman that needeth not to be ashamed, rightly dividing the word of truth.
> — 2 Timothy 2:15

1. Jude prayed that God's *peace* would be multiplied in our lives — that internal wars would cease, order would replace chaos, and a time for rebuilding would be ushered in. According to Paul's words in Philippians 4:6-8, how can you experience this calm, inner stability — even during circumstances that would normally be traumatic or upsetting?

2. When Jude called his readers "beloved," he used the term *agapetoi*. He did this to say that we, as believers, should view one another with deep admiration, awe, and wonder. How do you typically see other believers? As your brothers and sisters in Christ? Your competition? How does Scripture say we need to treat each other as members of God's family? (Consider First Peter 4:8; Ephesians 4:32; Philippians 2:1-5; and First John 4:7-12.)

3. Jude also uses the word *agonidzomai* as he's talking about how we need to contend for the faith, taking the challenge of living for Jesus as seriously as wrestlers do a professional match. This struggle isn't always with others; where else is it? (Read Paul's words in Romans 7:15-25, Ephesians 6:10-20; and Second Corinthians 10:3-5.)

PRACTICAL APPLICATION

> But be ye doers of the word, and not hearers only, deceiving your own selves.
> —James 1:22

Peter and Jude were deeply gripped by the need to help people know the truth of God's Word so they could recognize and escape the damage of following false teachers. They knew that the consequences of not knowing truth were dire — both then and now. Although false teaching may look different than it did in biblical times, one common way it shows up in modern life is through cults and/or the abuse of the position of a spiritual leader.

1. Do you know of anyone personally who's been affected by a cult or had a leader twist teaching for their own gain?
2. What does their situation show you about the value of knowing God's Word for yourself and asking Him for discernment when things become gray?
3. Is there an aspect of Scripture that you're especially passionate about? What do you want to make sure people understand accurately? Ask God to show you how to harness that passion to help others grasp the truth of His Word better.

LESSON 4

TOPIC

God's Expectation for Us To Maintain the Purity of the Faith

SCRIPTURES

1. **Jude 3** — Beloved, when I gave all diligence to write unto you of the common salvation, it was needful for me to write unto you, and exhort you that ye should earnestly contend for the faith which was once delivered unto the saints.

GREEK WORDS

1. "beloved" — ἀγαπητοί (*agapetoi*): plural version of ἀγάπη (*agape*) used to describe one's deep love for others; beloved; as with ἀγάπη (*agape*) it describes the admiration one has for an object of beauty; depicts an observer who experiences a loss of words to express what he feels because he is so taken with the beauty of an object or person; Jude used ἀγαπητοί (*agapetoi*) to mean we, as believers, should view one another with deep admiration, awe, and wonder

2. "diligence" — σπουδάζω (*spoudadzo*): to do something with eagerness; to do something with diligence; acting responsibly, quickly, and with attentiveness; one so diligent, excited, and energetic that he puts his whole heart into the principle or task before him; to do something with excitement, enthusiasm, and haste because it is so important, serious, or urgent; to give one's best efforts to a project or task and to do it enthusiastically; this word informs us Jude was excited about his plan to write an epistle about salvation and all of its mutually shared benefits

3. "common" — κοινός (*koinos*): what is commonly or mutually shared; could denote shared property or the benefits of a shared relationship; by using κοινός (*koinos*), Jude acknowledged that salvation has many benefits that mutually belong to all believers

4. "salvation" — σωτηρία (*soteria*): salvation; deliverance, healing, preservation, prosperity, safety, and general welfare

5. "needful" — ἀνάγκη (*anagke*): an urgent necessity
6. "exhort" — παρακαλέω (*parakaleo*): often used in ancient times to depict military leaders who came alongside their troops to urge, exhort, beseech, beg, and plead with them to stand tall and face their battles bravely
7. "earnestly contend" — ἐπαγωνίζομαι (*epagonidzomai*): a compound of ἐπί (*epi*) and ἀγωνίζομαι (*agonidzomai*); the preposition ἐπί (*epi*) means for or over, and it is used as an intensifier in the word ἐπαγωνίζομαι (*epagonidzomai*); the word ἀγωνίζομαι (*agonidzomai*) denotes an intense struggle and is where we derive the word "agony"; it was used to picture two wrestlers who agonized to win over the other in a wrestling match; both wrestlers worked to gain the advantage and hurl their opponent to the ground, exerting every ounce of their strength and skill to win a very intense physical contest; when ἐπί (*epi*) and ἀγωνίζομαι (*agonidzomai*) are compounded into a single word, it depicts those who are fighting with all of their might to win a match of some type, agonizing over it; Jude's use of this word means he was urging his readers to intensely fight over an issue or to fight for a truth
8. "once" — ἅπαξ (*hapax*): completion, finality, or something so complete that it needs nothing more to be added to it
9. "delivered" — παραδίδωμι (*paradidomi*): a compound of the preposition παρα (*para*) and δίδωμι (*didomi*); παρα (*para*) means along, as to pass something from one to the other, and the word δίδωμι (*didomi*) means to hand over, to pass to another, to transmit, or to transfer; in this verse, it means to deliver over to someone or to entrust to someone for their safekeeping, for example, as one would pass a tradition from one generation to another

SYNOPSIS

Isn't it amazing how Jude's letter — which was written nearly 2,000 years ago — can still be relevant today? It just goes to prove, "History merely repeats itself. Nothing is truly new; it has all been done or said before" (Ecclesiastes 1:9 *TLB*). The fact is believers today need to be just as on guard against false teachers and false doctrine as they were back then. We who have ears to hear would be wise to learn from Jude's telling revelation and heed his charge to "earnestly contend for the faith."

The emphasis of this lesson:

Jude was overwhelmed with love for the believers he was writing to and wanted more than anything for their faith to remain strong and pure in Christ. As he urged them to contend for their faith, he painted a picture of what it looks like — both for them and for us — and the picture is one of a diligent, wholehearted and energetic fighter bent on overcoming his opponent.

As Believers, We Are To View Each Other in Deep Admiration, Awe, and Wonder

Immediately after greeting and encouraging his readers, Jude dives into the purpose for his writing by saying:

> **Beloved, when I gave all diligence to write unto you of the common salvation, it was needful for me to write unto you, and exhort you that ye should earnestly contend for the faith which was once delivered unto the saints.**
> —Jude 3

There are several key words in this passage that are very important. For example, Jude addressed his readers as "beloved." In Greek, this is the word *agapetoi*, which is the plural form of *agape*, the term for the love of God. There are several words in Greek that are not easily translatable because they are so rich in meaning. *Agape* is one of them. Nevertheless, the base meaning of the word *agape* is: *One's deep love for a person or an object that causes an observer to experience a loss of words to express what he feels because he is so taken with the beauty of an object or person.* Here, Jude used *agapetoi* — translated as "beloved" — to instruct us as believers to view one another with deep admiration, awe, and wonder.

Jude Eagerly Wanted To Write About the Gift of Salvation

Jude goes on to say, "...When I gave all diligence to write unto you..." (Jude 3). We learned that the word "diligence" is a form of the Greek word *spoudadzo*, which means *to do something with eagerness or diligence*. It pictures *one so diligent, excited, and energetic that he puts his whole heart into the principle or task before him*. It signifies *doing something with excitement, enthusiasm, and haste because it is so important, serious, or urgent*. Moreover, this word *spoudadzo* means to give one's best efforts to a project or task and to do it enthusiastically. Jude's use of this word was the equivalent of him saying, "I was excited and fully intended on doing this."

What was he so enthusiastic about doing? He said, "…To write unto you of the common salvation…" (Jude 3). The word "common" here is the Greek word *koinos*, which describes *something that is commonly or mutually shared*. It is the very word that was used to denote *property mutually shared by a husband and wife*. In this case, Jude wanted to write about the many benefits of "salvation" mutually shared among all believers. This word "salvation" is a form of the Greek word *soteria*, which reflects the whole Jewish concept of salvation. Yes, it includes being saved from sin and going to Heaven, but it also includes *present deliverance, healing, preservation, prosperity, safety, and general welfare*. It was all these amazing benefits that we have by being placed in Christ that Jude was excited (*spoudadzo*) to write about.

Keep in mind, Jude was the half-brother of Jesus, the long-awaited Messiah. He was thrilled beyond words to think about all his older brother had accomplished through His life. He was the Lamb of God who died on the Cross to take away the sin of the world, and three days later was raised back to life! Jude was simply beaming with joy and enthusiasm to talk about all that our salvation entails.

Something Troubling Caused Jude To Change the Focus of His Letter

Then something happened that abruptly changed his plans. History reveals that Jude had gotten ahold of Peter's second letter and read it. Actually, it was a common practice for the apostles to read each other's writing (*see* 2 Peter 3:15,16). When Jude read about the false prophets who were teaching and trying to disseminate lies among believers, he was deeply disturbed. In fact, Jude was so troubled he wrote, "…It was needful for me to write unto you, and exhort you that ye should earnestly contend for the faith…" (Jude 3).

In Greek, the word "needful" is a translation of the word *anagke*, which describes *something urgent* or *a deep-felt need*. By using this word, Jude is letting us know that what Peter wrote was quite serious. He respected Peter greatly and felt compelled to "exhort" believers on the same subject. This word "exhort" is a form of the Greek word *parakaleo*, a compound of the word *para*, which means *to come alongside*, and the word *kaleo*, which means *to call out* or *to beckon*. *Parakaleo* is so strong it could be translated as *urge*, *beg*, *implore*, or even *pray*.

What's interesting is that in ancient times, the word *parakaleo* was used to depict military leaders who came alongside their troops to urge, exhort, beseech, beg, and plead with them to hold their head high, throw their shoulders back, and march forward into battle bravely to fight and win. Seeing how precarious the situation was, Jude knew someone needed to raise their voice like a commander and speak to the troops in the Body of Christ. Being the half-brother of Jesus, Jude seized his influence and exhorted (*parakaleo*) the believers to "…earnestly contend for the faith…" (Jude 3).

We Are To 'Earnestly Contend for the Faith'

The words "earnestly contend" are a compound of the Greek words *epi* and *agonidzomai*. The word *epi* is a preposition meaning *for* or *over* and is an intensifier of the word *agonidzomai*, which describes *an intense struggle* and is where we get the word "agony." When these words are combined to form *epagonidzomai*, it means *to earnestly agonize over something*. It is a picture of two wrestlers who agonize to win over the other in a wrestling match. Both wrestlers work to gain the advantage and hurl their opponent to the ground, exerting every ounce of their strength and skill to win a very intense physical contest.

In Jude's letter, the word *epagonidzomai* depicts the wrestling match between those standing for truth and their opponents who were pushing deception. False teachers were trying to wrestle faith to the ground, subdue it, and modify it to further their own agenda. As deception was wrestling to overpower truth, Jude said, "Earnestly contend (*epagonidzomai*) for the faith." In Greek, the phrase "the faith" includes a definite article, which means this is not just faith for healing or for miracles or for financial provision. This is "the faith" — *the clear, sound teaching of Scripture.*

Friend, every generation of believers is called by God to earnestly contend for the faith — including ours. With His grace empowering us, we are to fight for, defend, and guard the purity of the truth.

We Are To Preserve the Scriptures and Pass Them to the Next Generation

Jude tells us clearly that the truth we're fighting to preserve "…was once delivered unto the saints" (Jude 3). The Greek word for "once" here is *hapax*, and it describes *something that is complete or final*. In fact, it is so complete that it needs no modifications or anything more added to it. Thus, when the Bible was written, compiled, and delivered to us, it was complete.

This brings us to the word "delivered," which is a form of the Greek *paradidomi*, a compound of the preposition *para* and the word *didomi*. The word *para* means *along*, as *to pass something from one to the other*, and the word *didomi* means *to hand over, to pass to another, to transmit*, or *to transfer*. Jude uses this word to indicate the *delivery or passing of the Scriptures from one person to another, entrusting them to someone for their safekeeping*.

The passing on of family traditions would be a perfect example of this word *paradidomi*. Just as we share and pass on our Thanksgiving and Christmas traditions with our children as they grow up, we are to share and pass on the pure truth of God's Word with each upcoming generation. To be successful, we must be very intentional and seek to preserve the purity and integrity of the Scriptures as they were originally written, with nothing added or taken away.

Taking into account the original Greek meaning of all these words, here is the *Renner Interpretive Version (RIV)* of this part of Jude 3:

> **Beloved — I call you that because it's the only word I know to express how deeply I love and cherish you — I fully intended to write to you about our mutually shared salvation, and I was eager to write about this exciting subject, ready to engage all my creative abilities to dive deep into all the benefits that our salvation entails. But as I was about to get started, I found myself gripped with a sense of urgency and a deeply felt need to address another subject that came to my attention. I felt someone needed to come alongside the troops — to urge them to hold their head high, to throw their shoulders back and, if needed, to look the enemy eyeball to eyeball and to earnestly contend for the faith because it is under assault. God entrusted the faith to us once and for all and expects us to guard it and**

maintain its integrity in the same form it was delivered to us. God has given us the responsibility to impart it to others in the same form as when we received it.

Who Were These Ungodly Men?

So just how did these false teachers make their way into the Church, and what exactly were they doing? Jude tells us in verse 4: "For there are certain men crept in unawares, who were before of old ordained to this condemnation, ungodly men, turning the grace of our God into lasciviousness, and denying the only Lord God, and our Lord Jesus Christ."

What did Jude mean when he said that they "crept in unawares" and that they were "ordained to this condemnation"? What is "lasciviousness," and what would cause a person to "deny the only Lord God, our Lord Jesus Christ"? We will answer these questions and others in our final lesson.

STUDY QUESTIONS

> Study to shew thyself approved unto God, a workman that needeth not to be ashamed, rightly dividing the word of truth.
> — 2 Timothy 2:15

1. At the beginning, middle, and end of the Bible, God issues a strong warning concerning the way we handle and teach His Word — what is it? (Hint: check out Deuteronomy 4:2; Proverbs 30:5,6; and Revelation 22:18,19.)
2. God also promises to bless us in specific ways when we believe and follow His Word. What are some of those promises? (Consider Second Timothy 3:16,17; Psalm 18:30; 19:7-11; 107:8,9; 119:105; John 8:31,32; 15:7; and Romans 10:11.)
3. God wants us to view other believers with *deep admiration*, *awe*, and *wonder*. Can you imagine what it would be like if we all began to see and treat each other as precious, loved brothers and sisters? How many arguments could we avoid? What kind of restoration would take place? How many needs would be met? Read Acts 4:32-35 for a picture of what this kind of love and care produced in the Early Church.

PRACTICAL APPLICATION

> But be ye doers of the word, and not hearers only,
> deceiving your own selves.
> —James 1:22

1. As you've probably already seen, there is massive pressure from all sides to dilute the truth and compromise our faith in these last days. What aspects of truth have you felt pressured to hide, minimize, or renounce in order to be accepted and not criticized by others?
2. God has called us to preserve the purity and power of His Words and help pass them on to the next generation, but in order to be successful in this, we must be intentional. What are some ways that other believers have been intentional to help you know and stay true to Scripture?
3. On that note, who do you know that's younger than you in their walk with Jesus? How can you help them understand and apply God's Word accurately?

LESSON 5

TOPIC

Divine Warnings

SCRIPTURES

1. **Jude 3,4** — Beloved, when I gave all diligence to write unto you of the common salvation, it was needful for me to write unto you, and exhort you that ye should earnestly contend for the faith which was once delivered unto the saints. For there are certain men crept in unawares, who were before of old ordained to this condemnation, ungodly men, turning the grace of our God into lasciviousness, and denying the only Lord God, and our Lord Jesus Christ.
2. **2 Peter 2:1-6** — But there were false prophets also among the people, even as there shall be false teachers among you, who privily shall bring in damnable heresies, even denying the Lord that bought them, and bring upon themselves swift destruction. And many shall follow their pernicious ways; by reason of whom the way of truth shall be evil spoken of. And through covetousness shall they with feigned words make

merchandise of you: whose judgment now of a long time lingereth not, and their damnation slumbereth not. For if God spared not the angels that sinned, but cast them down to hell, and delivered them into chains of darkness, to be reserved unto judgment; And spared not the old world, but saved Noah the eighth person, a preacher of righteousness, bringing in the flood upon the world of the ungodly; And turning the cities of Sodom and Gomorrah into ashes condemned them with an overthrow, making them an ensample unto those that after should live ungodly.

GREEK WORDS

1. "crept in unawares" — παρεισδύω (*pareisduo*): a triple compound of παρά (*para*), εἰς (*eis*), and δύνω (*duno*); the preposition παρά (*para*) means alongside, the word εἰς (*eis*) means into, and δύνω (*duno*) means to enter and settle down into a place; compounded, it pictures those who clandestinely enter into a certain place and who settle down and function right alongside of others; covert activity
2. "before of old" — πάλαι (*palai*): long ago, in times past, or in former times
3. "ordained" — προγράφω (*prographo*): a compound of πρό (*pro*) and γράφω (*grapho*); the preposition πρό (*pro*) means before or in advance and the word γράφω (*grapho*) means I write; as a compound, something that has been clearly foretold and written in advance, thus, an advanced written warning
4. "condemnation" — κρίμα (*krima*): a damning verdict of judgment and condemnation; a judicial verdict of judgment
5. "ungodly men" — ἀσεβής (*asebes*): from σεβής (*sebes*), reverent, pious, respectful, God-fearing; when an ἀ (*a*) is attached to it, the prefix has a canceling or reversing effect; what was once holy has become unholy, those who were once reverent have become irreverent, what was once God-fearing has lost its fear of God; irreverent or disrespectful and depicts those who have lost their fear of God and those whose deeds are unholy, unsacred, impure, and whose activities are unsanctioned by God
6. "turning" — μετατίθημ (*metatithimi*): a compound of μετά (*meta*) and τίθημι (*tithemi*); the preposition μετά (*meta*) denotes a change and τίθημι (*tithemi*) means to place or to position; in this verse, the

word pictures an alteration, change, or modification of a position or a truth

7. "lasciviousness" — ἀσέλγεια (*aselgeia*): indulgent sinful excess that is especially marked by sexual depravity, the removal of sexual restraints, and gluttony along with other base activities; it is the same word used in Second Peter 2:7 where it is listed as the principal sin of Sodom and Gomorrah and the reason for God's judgment upon those cities

8. "lord" — δεσπότης (*despotes*): an administrative term that normally referred to one like a chief executive officer or one with authority over others in the executive department directly under his control; a technical term to describe the chief steward of large households who had authority over all the other servants in a household; those under such a "lord" reported to him, received instructions from him, were paid by him, and, if the need arose, they were dismissed by him; same word used in Second Peter 2:1

9. "denying" — ἀρνέομαι (*arneomai*): to knowingly deny; to knowingly disown; to knowingly reject; to knowingly refuse; or to knowingly renounce; one who knowingly disavows, forsakes, walks away from, or washes one's hands of another person or group of people; depicts something done with one's full consent and understanding of what is being done; as used at this juncture, this category of erring individuals were knowingly rejecting the authority of the Lord and they knowingly ignored the warning signals given to them by the Holy Spirit

SYNOPSIS

In Lessons 3 and 4, we unpacked the meaning of Jude 3, where he said, "Beloved, when I gave all diligence to write unto you of the common salvation, it was needful for me to write unto you, and exhort you that ye should earnestly contend for the faith which was once delivered unto the saints."

Taking into account the original Greek meaning of the key words in this passage, here once again is the *Renner Interpretive Version (RIV)* of Jude 3:

> **Beloved — I call you that because it's the only word I know to express how deeply I love and cherish you — I fully intended to write to you about our mutually shared salvation, and I was eager to write about this exciting subject, ready to engage all my creative abilities to dive deep into all the benefits that our**

salvation entails. But as I was about to get started, I found myself gripped with a sense of urgency and a deeply felt need to address another subject that came to my attention. I felt someone needed to come alongside the troops — to urge them to hold their head high, to throw their shoulders back and, if needed, to look the enemy eyeball to eyeball and to earnestly contend for the faith because it is under assault. God entrusted the faith to us once and for all and expects us to guard it and maintain its integrity in the same form it was delivered to us. God has given us the responsibility to impart it to others in the same form as when we received it.

Peter's Warning About False Teachers Deeply Disturbed Jude

What came to Jude's attention that was so alarming he felt the urgency to address another subject? It was Peter's second letter written to First Century believers. In it he said, "But there were false prophets also among the people, even as there shall be false teachers among you, who privily shall bring in damnable heresies, even denying the Lord that bought them, and bring upon themselves swift destruction" (2 Peter 2:1).

Peter not only spoke about false prophets infiltrating the Church in his day, but also in the days to come. Speaking futuristically, he said there *shall be* false teachers throughout the Church Age. How much influence and impact will these deceitful leaders have? Peter said:

> And many shall follow their pernicious ways; by reason of whom the way of truth shall be evil spoken of. And through covetousness shall they with feigned words make merchandise of you: whose judgment now of a long time lingereth not, and their damnation slumbereth not.
> — 2 Peter 2:2,3

There are many similar warnings throughout the New Testament regarding false teachers, false prophets, and those who speak falsehoods. Anytime someone misrepresents the truth about God's Word, about themselves, or about someone or something else for their personal benefit, the Bible says they are speaking "lies." That's what these pseudo prophets and teachers were doing — and would do again — and God's judgment was already on its way. Peter gave these examples of how God dealt with such individuals in the past:

> **For if God spared not the angels that sinned, but cast them down to hell, and delivered them into chains of darkness, to be reserved unto judgment;**
>
> **And spared not the old world, but saved Noah the eighth person, a preacher of righteousness, bringing in the flood upon the world of the ungodly;**
>
> **And turning the cities of Sodom and Gomorrah into ashes condemned them with an overthrow, making them an ensample unto those that after should live ungodly.**
>
> — 2 Peter 2:4-6

It was these words from Peter that moved Jude to change the focus of his letter and build on what Peter had written. Again, taking into account the original Greek meaning, here once again is the *Renner Interpretive Version (RIV)* of the latter part of Jude 3:

> …I felt someone needed to come alongside the troops — to urge them to hold their head high, to throw their shoulders back and, if needed, to look the enemy eyeball to eyeball and to earnestly contend for the faith because it is under assault. God entrusted the faith to us once and for all and expects us to guard it and maintain its integrity in the same form it was delivered to us. God has given us the responsibility to impart it to others in the same form as when we received it.

The emphasis of this lesson:

Like Peter, Jude warned his readers of ungodly individuals who had stealthily wormed their way into the Church. This had been prophesied by the Holy Spirit from ancient times. These men who were once reverent and holy became irreverent, unholy, and no longer feared God. They perverted God's grace and opened the door to sinful excess — especially in the area of sexual depravity. In spite of God's warnings to repent and return to the truth, they rejected His authority.

Certain Men 'Crept in Unawares'

When we come to Jude 4, we see that Jude begins to zero in on what these false teachers were doing. He said, "For there are certain men crept in unawares, who were before of old ordained to this condemnation, ungodly men, turning the grace of our God into lasciviousness, and denying the only Lord God, and our Lord Jesus Christ."

Notice the phrase "crept in unawares." It is a translation of the Greek word *pareisduo*, which is a triple compound of the words *para*, *eis*, and *duno*. The preposition *para* means *alongside*; the word *eis* means *into*; and the word *duno* means *to enter and settle down into a place*. When these three words are compounded to form *pareisduo*, it pictures *those who clandestinely enter into a certain place and who settle down and function right alongside of others*. In this case, it is covert activity of individuals who have craftily wormed their way right into the ranks of the Church.

Here again, we see Jude reiterating what he read in Second Peter 2:1. In Peter's letter, however, he used the Greek word *pareisago*, which is a little different from the word Jude used. The word *pareisago* is a compound of the word *para*, meaning *alongside*; the word *eis*, meaning *into* and carries the idea of *penetration*; and the word *ago*, meaning *I lead*. Taken together, the word *pareisago* seems to picture *those who have leadership positions in the Church who were covertly bringing in false doctrine*.

When we take into account Jude's use of the word *pareisduo*, the *Renner Interpretive Version (RIV)* of the beginning of Jude 4 would be:

> **Unfortunately, we are now confronted with a certain category of individuals who have clandestinely, almost like a stealth operation, craftily wormed their way right into the middle of our ranks...**

The Holy Spirit Warned Us of These Perpetrators in Advance

Jude went on to say that these pretenders and purveyors of lies "…were before of old ordained to this condemnation…" (Jude 4). The phrase "before of old" in Greek is *palai*, which means *long ago, in times past*, or *in former times*. Keep in mind, the Holy Spirit is prompting Jude what to write. Thus, the fact that the word *palai* is used here tells us the Spirit of

God has been prophesying that these false teachers would be coming since the beginning.

When Jude said these evildoers were "ordained," he used the Greek word *prographo*, which is a compound of the words *pro* and *grapho*. The word *pro* is a preposition meaning *before* or *in advance*, and the word *grapho* means *I write*. When these words are compounded to form *prographo*, it describes *something that has been clearly foretold and written in advance*; thus, *an advanced written warning*. The fact is God gave us written notification during ancient times that false teachers would arise at the end of the age. As we read further into Jude's letter, we will see that he's quoting Enoch who was the seventh from Adam and considered to be one of the earliest prophets in the Old Testament.

Jude said these deceptive individuals were ordained to this "condemnation." In Greek, the word "condemnation" is *krima*, and it describes *a damning verdict of judgment and condemnation* or *a judicial verdict of judgment*. Basically, this verse informs us that God will investigate the activities of those who use their spiritual influence incorrectly and will judge them accordingly. Hence, the Judge of the earth is watching at all times, observing this category of errant leaders, and in the end, Heaven's court will issue a final verdict of judgment against them.

These 'Ungodly Men' Were Once Godly

It is important to note that Jude labels these false teachers as "ungodly men," which is the Greek word *asebes*. It is derived from the word *sebes*, which means *reverent, pious, respectful*, and *God-fearing*. When an "a" is attached to it, the prefix has a canceling or reversing effect. In other words, what was once holy has become *unholy*; those who were once reverent have become *irreverent*; and what was once God-fearing has *lost its fear of God*. Thus, the word *asebes* — translated here as "ungodly men" — speaks of *irreverent* or *disrespectful individuals* and depicts *those who have lost their fear of God and those whose deeds are unholy, unsacred, impure, and whose activities are unsanctioned by God*.

This is a picture of people who have veered from their faith. Although they began as reverent, holy, and respectful people who had a healthy fear of God, now they have embraced a new doctrine and have become irreverent, unholy, disrespectful, and have lost their fear of the Lord. In fact, these individuals degenerated to such an extent that Jude says they were "…turning the grace of our God into lasciviousness…" (Jude 4).

The word "turning" here is the Greek word *metatithimi*, which is a compound of the words *meta* and *tithemi*. The preposition *meta* denotes *a change*, and the word *tithemi* means *to place* or *to position*. Hence, the word *metatithimi* — translated as "turning" in this verse — pictures *an alteration, change,* or *modification of a position or a truth*. These ungodly men changed the way *they saw and taught about the grace of God*, and that modification led to *lasciviousness*.

In Greek, the word "lasciviousness" is a translation of the word *aselgeia*, which depicts *indulgent, sinful excess that is especially marked by sexual depravity, the removal of sexual restraints*, and *gluttony* along with other *base activities*. It is the same word used in Second Peter 2:7 where it is listed as the principal sin of Sodom and Gomorrah and the reason for God's judgment upon those cities.

Essentially, Jude is telling us that when you twist and change the meaning of the grace of God, it opens the door for people to believe anything goes and anything is alright. This ultimately leads to *lasciviousness* — a twisted mindset that makes people think living immoral, indecent lives is okay because the grace of God covers them.

They Knowingly Rejected the Authority of the Lord

In addition to turning the grace of God into a license to sin, these ungodly men were also "…denying the only Lord God, and our Lord Jesus Christ" (Jude 4). Normally, when the word "Lord" is used in the New Testament, it is the Greek word *kurios*, which means *supreme lord and master* — one who has absolute authority and the final say. This is how every Christian would describe the Lordship of Jesus. However, in Jude 4 the word for Lord is not *kurios* but *despotes*.

The word *despotes* is an administrative term that normally referred to *one like a chief executive officer (CEO) of an organization* or *one with authority over others in the executive department directly under his control*. This was a technical term to describe *the chief steward of large households who had authority over all the other servants in a household*, and those under such a "lord" reported to him, received instructions from him, were paid by him, and, if the need arose, they were dismissed by him. This word *despotes* — translated here as "Lord" — is the same word used in Second Peter 2:1, where he talks about false prophets "denying the *Lord* that bought them."

By using this word *despotes* (Lord), Jude is describing those who have been genuinely called by Christ into positions of leadership in the Church. They relate to Jesus not only as their Savior, but also as their Chief Executive Officer who called them and placed them in their leadership role. Although they're answerable to the Lord, they are *denying* His explicit directions.

The word "denying" is a translation of the Greek word *arneomai*, which means *to knowingly deny, to knowingly disown, to knowingly reject, to knowingly refuse*, or *to knowingly renounce*. It refers to *one who knowingly disavows, forsakes, walks away from, or washes one's hands of another person or group of people*. Thus, it depicts *something done with one's full consent and understanding of what is being done*.

The fact that both Peter and Jude used this word *arneomai* — translated as "denying" — tells us that this category of erring individuals were knowingly rejecting the authority of the Lord and they knowingly ignored the warning signals given to them by the Holy Spirit. Therefore, they were not innocent because the Lord who is over them had spoken to them and had told them to change, but they refused to accept what He said to them.

Taking into account the original Greek meaning of the key words in this passage, here is the *Renner Interpretive Version (RIV)* of Jude 4:

> **Unfortunately, we are now confronted with a certain category of individuals who have clandestinely, almost like a stealth operation, craftily wormed their way right into the middle of our ranks. Long ago it was foretold and written in advance that a day would come when such individuals would show up. But in the end, Heaven's court will issue a damning verdict of judgment and condemnation on them due to their activities. I'm talking about people who were once reverent and God-fearing, but now they have obviously lost their fear of God. These are individuals who go about altering, changing, and modifying the grace of our God into a teaching that says everything is okay and that leads to sinful living that is especially marked by immoral and indecent sexual activities along with other base instincts. They can't claim ignorance about what they are**

doing because the Lord God, that is, our Lord Jesus Christ, has spoken to them and warned them to get back in line. But in spite of these warnings that the Lord has given them, they knowingly are denying and walking away from the authoritative covering of the Lord.

Jude Issues a Warning of Judgment

With a keen awareness of the activities and influence of the ungodly leadership that had stealthily made its way into the Church, Jude began issuing a strong warning to his readers. He said, "I will therefore put you in remembrance, though ye once knew this, how that the Lord, having saved the people out of the land of Egypt, afterward destroyed them that believed not" (Jude 5).

Those under corrupt leaders tend to mimic their corrupt behavior. Jude knew that when leaders change the grace of God into a "free pass" to sin, the people under their authority would do the same. We are seeing this happen in record numbers in the Church today. Many Christians think, *Well, I'm saved, and since I'm saved, I'm no longer living with the prospect of divine judgment; I've been removed from that.* Through Jude, the Holy Spirit warns us otherwise.

The first example of judgment he reminds us of is that of the children of Israel. God had intervened on their behalf and delivered them out of Egyptian bondage. Yet, although they were "saved," that didn't give them license to do anything they wanted. When they repeatedly disobeyed God and refused to trust His word, He judged them, which is what we see happening all through Scripture and where we will pick up in Part 2 of our study on the book of Jude.

STUDY QUESTIONS

> Study to shew thyself approved unto God, a workman that needeth not to be ashamed, rightly dividing the word of truth.
> — 2 Timothy 2:15

1. Jude said that the activity of false prophets was foretold by the Holy Spirit far in advance of their occurrence. That's how God works. He lets those close to Him know what is coming *before* it takes place. What promise does God make in these passages that encourages you

to get close and stay close to Him? (See Deuteronomy 29:29; Psalm 25:14; Amos 3:7; Daniel 2:22; John 15:15; 16:13-15; and First Corinthians 2:9,10.)

2. What is one thing you know without a doubt God revealed to you ahead of time? How did this divine revelation help you in your walk with Him?

3. Although some people believe they're getting away with their wrongdoing, they are mistaken. God is aware of all things at all times. What do these passages specifically say to confirm this powerful principle?

- **Hebrews 4:13; 1 John 3:20**
- **1 Chronicles 28:9; Jeremiah 17:10; Revelation 2:23**
- **Proverbs 15:3; Jeremiah 23:24**
- **Psalm 139:1-16**

4. According to Ezekiel 16:49 and 50, what was the root cause that led the people of Sodom and Gomorrah into sin? What does this say to you about your own life? How about the sins of our nation?

PRACTICAL APPLICATION

> But be ye doers of the word, and not hearers only,
> deceiving your own selves.
> —James 1:22

1. The "ungodly men" whom Jude described were once reverent, respectful individuals who had a healthy fear of God. But after listening to and embracing perverted teaching, they became irreverent, disrespectful, and unholy. Do you know anyone who has experienced such a negative transformation? What kind of demented doctrine did they latch on to and begin believing that took them down the wrong path? What can you learn from their example and apply in your life to avoid making the same mistake?

2. These ungodly men changed the way they saw and taught about the grace of God, and that modification led to *lasciviousness*, which is *indulgent sinful excess that is especially marked by sexual depravity, the removal of sexual restraints*, and *gluttony*. Where are you seeing this scenario play out in the church world today? What negative repercussions have resulted?

3. God's grace is not a great "cover-up" for sinful behavior. Rather, it is His supernatural power to avoid sinning. Where do you need God's grace most to overcome ungodly thinking and behavior? Pause and pray, asking the Holy Spirit to daily pour His grace into your life to live pure and holy. (Consider His promises in Second Corinthians 9:8; Psalm 84:11; James 4:6.)
4. Be honest: Are you honoring Jesus as "Lord" (*Kurios*) in your life? Is He your Supreme Master who has absolute authority? Or are you treating Him as "Lord" — *despotes* — your Chief Executive Officer whose authority you have turned a deaf ear to?

Notes

CLAIM YOUR FREE RESOURCE!

As a way of introducing you further to the teaching ministry of Rick Renner, we would like to send you free of charge his teaching CD, "How To Receive a Miraculous Touch From God."

In His earthly ministry, Jesus commonly healed *all* who were sick of *all* their diseases. In this profound message, learn about the manifold dimensions of Christ's wisdom, goodness, power, and love toward all humanity who came to Him in faith with their needs.

☑ **YES, I want to receive Rick Renner's monthly teaching letter!**

Simply scan the QR code to claim this resource or go to:
renner.org/claim-your-free-offer

WITH US!

 renner.org    facebook.com/rickrenner

 youtube.com/rennerministries    instagram.com/rickrrenner

www.ingramcontent.com/pod-product-compliance
Lightning Source LLC
Chambersburg PA
CBHW061257040426
42444CB00010B/2400